the UNIVERSE &
the mad BUTTERFLY

PRATISH MISTRY

mystic tree

a Mystic Tree book

Copyright © Pratish Mistry, 2006

With thanks to Light, Knowledge and Music

A CIP catalogue record for this book is available from the
British Library

Pratish Mistry is hereby identified as the author of this work
in accordance with Section 77 of the Copyright, Designs
and Patents Act 1988. Illustrations Copyright © Shilpashree
Balaram, 2006. Cover design by Mayur Mistry.

ISBN: 0-9553189-0-4

Printed and bound in the U.K.

to the quietly spiritual

illustrations by
shilpashree balaram

the universe
and the mad butterfly
teasing imperfection

Author's Note

Often the smallest of actions can trigger a sequence of events with ultimately a much greater impact. In chaos theory this is described as the Butterfly Effect and it is, for me, an observation of how the universe tends towards a state of balance.

The Universe & the Mad Butterfly is a collection of observations on life, nature and the world we live in. It is written in verse similar in form to the Japanese Senryu and describes how we move closer to an ultimate balance within ourselves.

The verses can be read as stand-alone, or as verses linked to each other in various ways. Different ways of reading them may give you quite distinct interpretations.

Appreciation of new perspectives and defining moments in our self-awareness usually arrive hand in hand. I hope that you enjoy the verses and that the different meanings you discover will guide you on your journey to wherever you want to be.

Pratish Mistry

Foreword

Dear Reader,

It gives me pleasure to introduce the writing of my fellow traveller. Written simply and with depth, I sincerely believe this work will hold importance for those who experience it and allow their minds to wander across its different meanings.

This butterfly reminds me of an old Buddhist story of a young man asleep in a field who dreams he is a butterfly. Until he wakes up and wonders if he is in reality just a butterfly dreaming that it is a man. There is so much inner confusion on the way to mindfulness but finally we become aware of the power of our minds, if that is what we want.

I hope you will consider this book as an exchange between travellers for it is frequently the strangest of words and strangers that allow us the most space to absorb both the new and the past.

Tenzing Rinpoche

with direction but for light
a random moth flutters
in delight

sunshine or rain,
an inspired world
smiles upon its muse

trapped melancholy
in an unlikely song
sings itself free

beauty for an instant
through a tattooed trunk
throwing triple twenty

red kites flying high
over bright toys on the ground
leave sly prey unfound

desire to repeat
a moment's happiness
trapped in primal curse

be longing well
as shortly it leaves itself
where it does not belong

.

a teardrop contained in a cloud
masks the sunshine
for an ant

too much happiness
slowly fades into darkness
leaving you blind

satisfaction of desire
merely puts it in touch
with its inner rabbit

in glorious slums
poor folk starved of light and stitch
ahhh... lives of the rich

in locked steel cages
behind traditional veils
creativity blossoms

little brother wants
to grow up to be a need
that can hardly be satisfied

happy is having nothing
but a life without wanting
keys to handcuffs

the powerless universe
                ultimately yields
                                to every desire

greedy toads
            get what they curse for
                        later nursing wasted wishes

                nature conspires
              to fulfil intentions
            when it feels like it

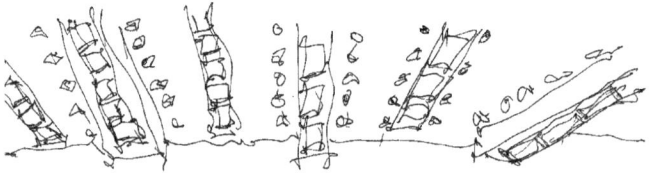

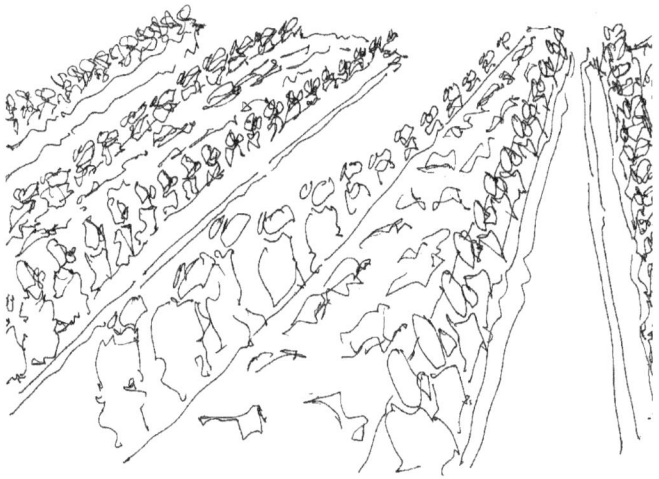

an arrow glides without scruple
as nature takes its course
in flight

                    lord of the supply chain
                    the universe delivers
                    just in time

her awkward, demure demeanour
suggests exciting sex, ahhh…
queen's gambit

she switches her focus off
and lures him into her trap
cruel ease

the owl blinked
a sleepy hello
to the early morning light

look!
look at the sun's rays
thinging through the thingie!

pleasing, familiar scent
on every breath
heads rest easy on pillows

friendship of truth and time
disappearing forever
in just an instant

these little reminders
that life is short
make worthy memories

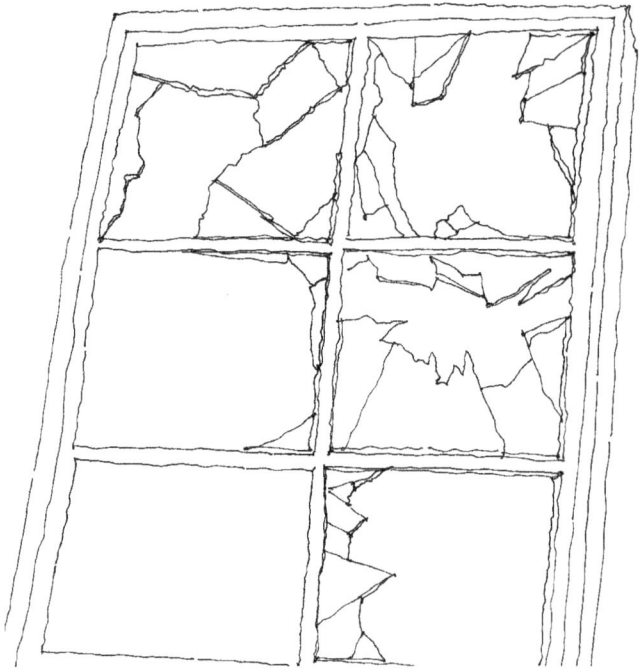

a stone cast
makes for a solid foundation
and ripples

options distract
the unsteady mind
to the point of total confusion

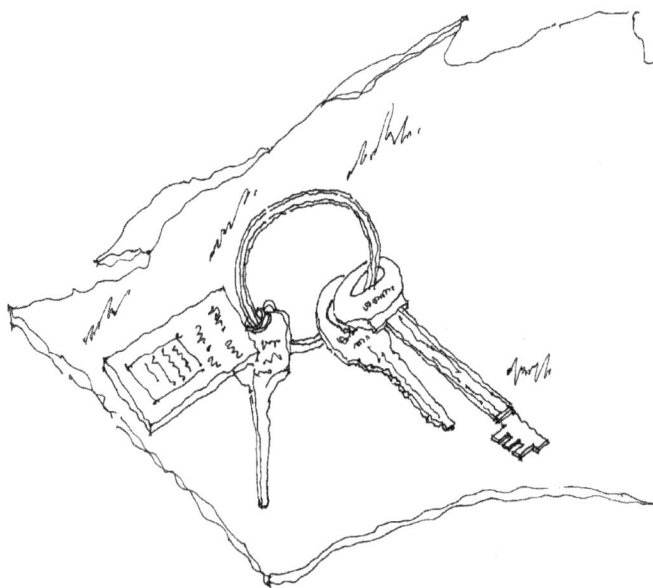

accepting souls small
as the world moves fast
toward the unknown for all

lovers part longing
that the uncertainty
would disappear

concentrate orange,
questions compel
answers to appear nearby

driven by nature
the tornado destroys
friends in his path

harsh rain of like stature
enriches enemies in her aftermath

an uncontrolled beast
lacks the ability
to step out of itself

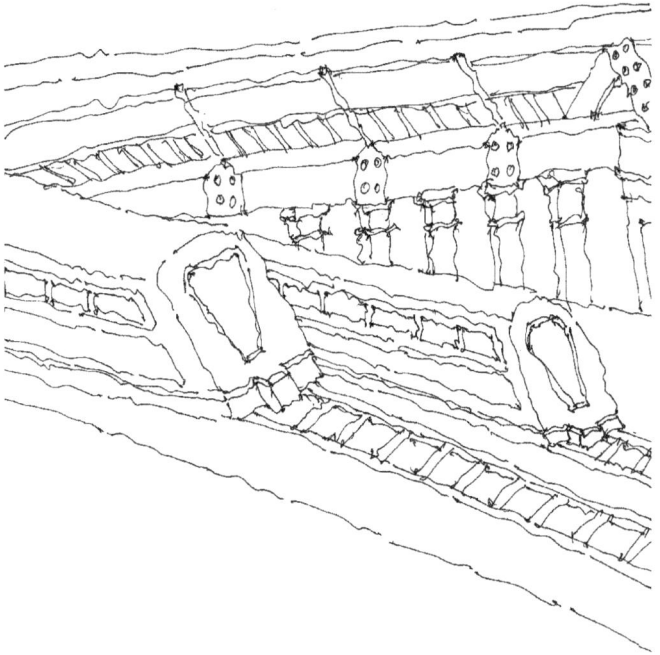

deny nature
for short term stature
until the primal returns to haunt

oh beautiful rose
in the depths of hell
stop whingeing and go home

searching for completion
misfit halves and quarters
find some lonely thirds

unlikely companions
having nothing in common
but the moment

"without you I am incomplete"
said the rose to its petal
innocent

"nonsense" replied the petal
"you would be a perfect rose,
just different."

nurtured misery
so naturally reveals
an awareness lost

with emotions high
the mind tries to stab and kill:
                    attempted murder

something silly said silently
rests in poor company
if allowed

the chair smiled and sucked it up
knowing the fat pig
would eventually stand

29

the eyes dull and die
  as a spirit being broken
    gives birth to a cynic

physical and mental divorce
  precedes a marriage
    with counsellors

feeling down and low
  she chisels self and hammers heart
    distant seems a new start

magical jade transforms
an otherwise pretty face
into a gargoyle

with life's love lost comes
a short dwelling in the past
strength, contract killer

gentle ja moon
bathing a jaded heart
with colour

a heart tormented
creates a lovely butterfly
with slightly greener wings

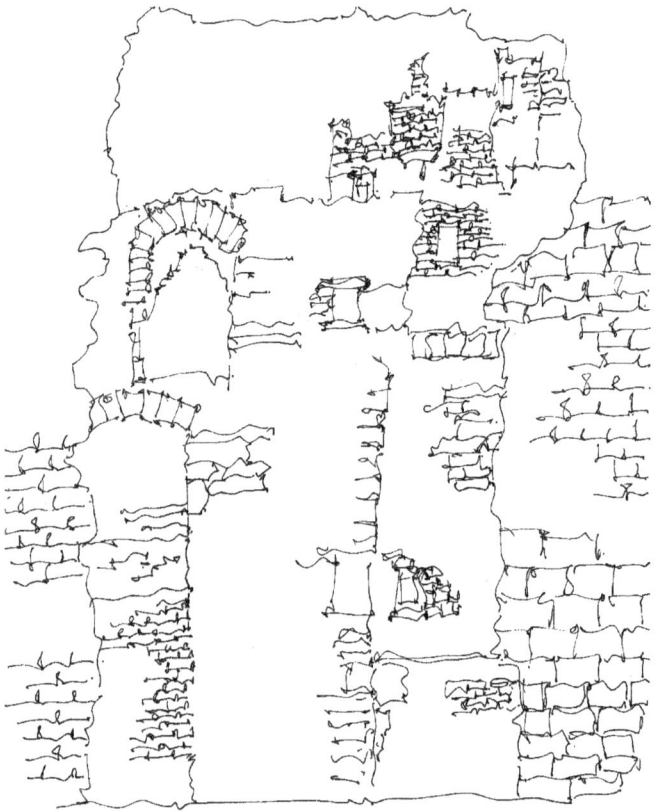

how the wise
and innocent mature
into a foetal bundle of fear

fires forge ahead
consuming hearts and minds
and spirits by choice

hard, worn stones cold
heard what they have been told
and misinterpreted

brahmins decree
tuna-safe dolphin
marine racism

with fuzzy logic
even rogue racoons
can be proven innocent

a woman possessed
with passionate talisman
relieved without dowry

spectacles
sometimes help realise
the loss of perspective

imagine a world
without structure or chaos
and observe how it works

a beautiful land of plenty
where kittens and puppies play,
carefree

o' skilful conductor,
circumstances surround
every distant sound

a universe impartial
does not get personal
there is just no time

the mind's conviction
is free to overpower
circumstance

absolute power is rare
but without a care,
it is available

a gentle breeze carried away
the air of unsettledness

old flame
as fire in nature
burns the flesh in spite of maturity

selfless and simple
compassionate breeze
easing discomfort with such ease

casual flirting glances
touch each other
for a moment

aware the busking guitarist
distracts innocent souls
and captures them in his web

a cautious kiss
leads express movement
hoping to still the mind

greed overcomes
some difficult obstacles
to become king

following false prophets
masses helplessly worship
the corporate idol

apparently bearable pain
in cubicles forced to produce
factory farming

airstrip myths say
it is tough to conquer
wanting fruits and fame

holding company
in high esteem
misguides the herd's loyalty

at the end
of a useful life
the fridge is left in the cold

a life destroyed
to make more money
sorry, poor tree

bear witness
to yourself in the bile farm
sleeping peacefully

        admire the ego
        elaborate peacocks
        express

as the pride roared
to the world's awe
the tree discovered inner peace

careering upward
without a care and prayer
oh for a timely puncture

daily reflection
mirrors a life behind bars
such alcoholism

choice stroke conditions
for a life without a voice
of reason or expression

cloud to my moon
revealing a silver
expression for an invisible man

pressing needs
obliged to remember
the only thing one has to do is die

what is done
with no lights and blind eyes
reveals some dark realities

facing a certain end
drink the half full glass
before emptying the mind

in the absence of security
live fast and die young
or let thoughts break you

nature leaves no choice
it knows the route for all journeys afoot,
bar small detours

such deep sorrow
quenching the earth's thirst
eats where there is no appetite

open minds accept
what fists cannot embrace,
baby steps Muhammad Ali

patience is the key
so breathe calmly, wait and see
what size fits the lock

the world doesn't care
whether you think
you're in control

how things change
a life and moment ephemeral
too bad so sad

gently swaying shafts
bending with the times
survive serial killers

a blue moon rising
over barren lands
is rarely more than a blemish

fickle winds
plague the shores
raising spirits from stubborn claws

the deep pain and torture
of hope and kidney stones
this too shall pass

the thought factory
manufactures misery
with products of your choice

in vast, open plains
herds without complement
are lost in migration

modern-day pharaoh
with no followers but one
how will you face death?

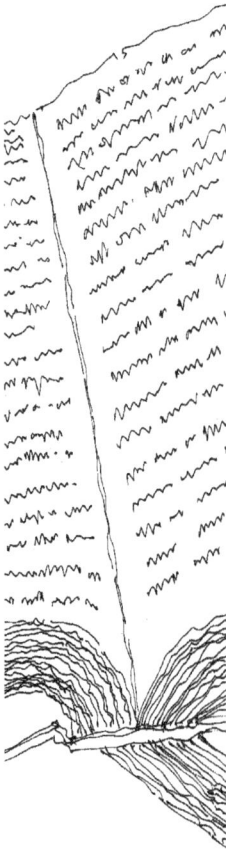

lust for meaning
is a fair swap
in the absence of purpose

how irrelevant
is a pretty rainbow
from a water sprinkler?

glorious energy
harnessed to ponder
if lima beans come from peru

loneliness abounds
for the solitary mind
that had too much time to think

on days like today
I like to remind myself
of happy things

gods and devils
in imaginary pursuit
thrive in their own reality

lighting incense
carries scented wafts
to those who breathe

fifty one finally knows
who fifty is
after passing him

silent stays the master
whose compass is hidden
from those who cannot see

stereotypes
based on a sample of one
are statistically significant

magicians conjure images
kings and lovers adore
reality redefined, as never before

pop psychology
makes sunshine where
intellect sadly reigns supreme

awaken the dwarf within
and feel the art of loving
the Great Cornholio

strategy composers
fail to solve mysteries
for carpenters are the tools

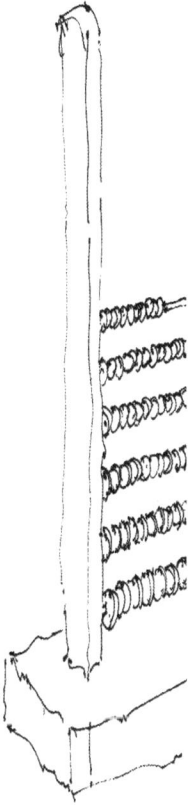

the stressful life
of a destiny mastered
by a weak mind

exploring a body
of shallow water
requires some depth

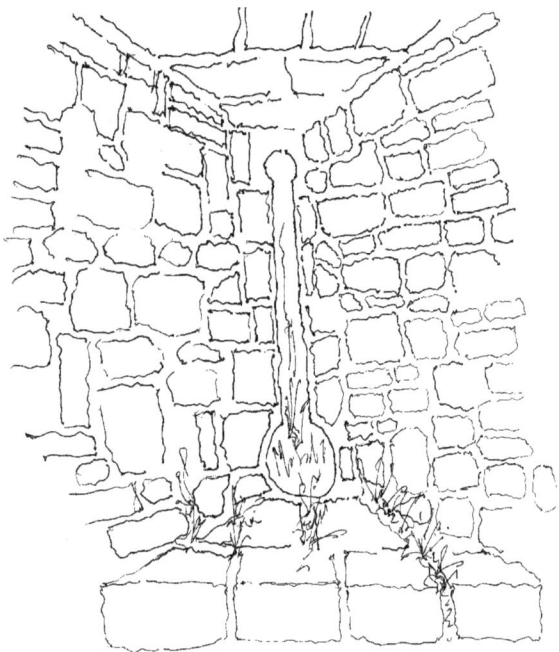

that old lady
with the funny hair
hides unfathomable secrets

the rock spoke in a strange language
saying some stupid things
I did not know

raindrops dance
a classical dance
when no one is watching

in a sea of options
sanity treads and paddles
until it drowns

for those moments
in which I am so present
that I am somewhere else

proceed with caution,
there are good things waiting
around the next corner

weeks of ingenuity
for a second's work,
fortune or ruin

bending moments
ultimately break
as tension builds without relief

spirits having flown
claiming independence
rest uneasy in company

an image projected
influences the world
to return the favour

belief ignites
a self-fulfilling prophecy
that otherwise need not be

a welcome invitation
as fear will always be near,
waiting for you

securely padlocked
box of fear and doubt
neatly picked by a thought

acting on blind intuition
is smarter than you think
if you know what you're doing

                    thinking positively
                    deceives the mind
                    helping or hindering fear

in intuition
grows a basic rationale
waiting to be born

moving beetles turn
like resting jaguars cannot
smart power steering

breaking an unwritten law
he untied the normal
shoelace

even nature
has to conquer inertia
to gather its direction

time slows
as the body acts freely
beyond the mind's pondering

thoughts and perspectives
to help you rationalise
what wasted effort

a climax of intuition
followed by months
of reasonable foreplay

the sparrow
flapped its wings indifferently
and uplifted itself

the truth outlives
whatever gets you through the night
wake up stubborn bitch!

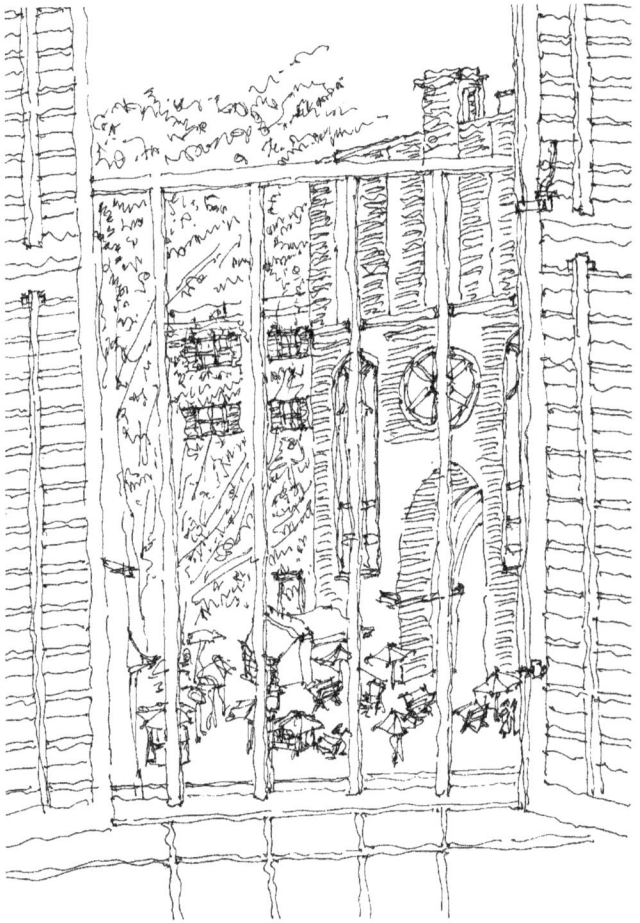

what a struggle:
each dark, grey cloud holds
raindrops waiting to break free

ordinary people roam the zoo
oblivious of the animals
that they are

actions free of desire
escape from expectation's guard
to strangely fulfil

carving through virgin forest
confident souls find themselves
amongst demons

life is full of people
who know what one needs
maybe one is an idiot

pirates of unchartered paths
use random maps
on which y marks the spot

backing solid rock
it pays to know
there is music for all persuasions

much future action
stems from an old seed,
unaware of its presence

a prisoner escapes
from rules clouding judgement,
the monsoon of freedom

a mind running wild
experiencing liberty
outside society

a river overflows
destroying banks and the mind
drowns rational thought

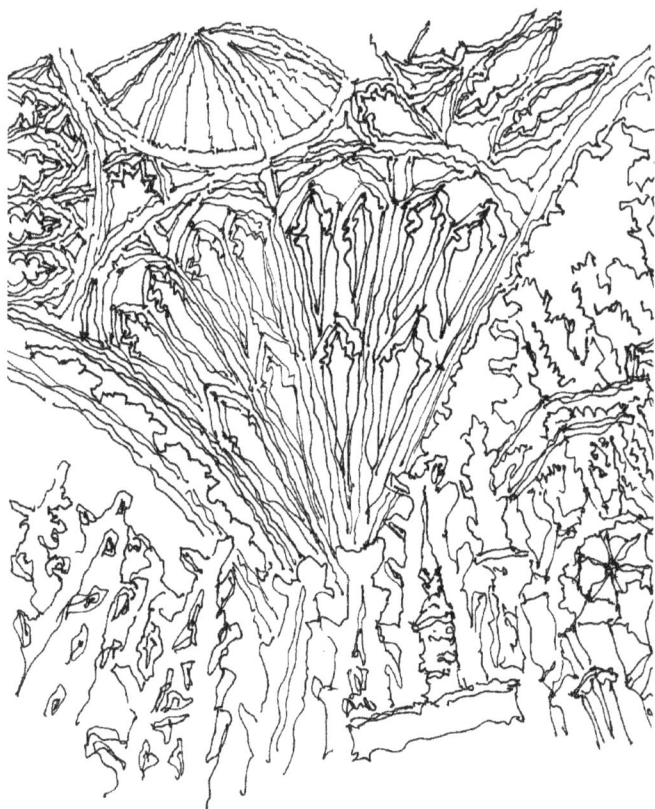

there is so much noise
that a mind cannot even see
ambiguity

in practice, knowing
which questions are relevant
leads to the answer

step back
to have a closer look
at the puzzle's noisy detail

for a still moment
as an angel
at peace with the world

water calms
banks renew and born are palms
to an irrigated mind

on a lonely planet
battling causes so just
me against the world

mind the rapid
that overpowers rafts
as they head for a waterfall

after futile preparation
the twig surrenders control
and goes with the flow

an element of choice
directs the perception
of yourself and others

with cards never shown
surrender to the unknown
can help win a hand

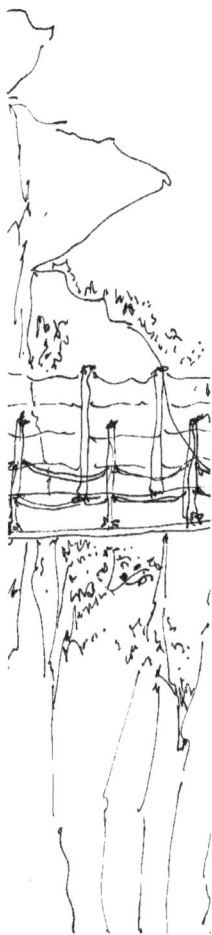

brave,
sometimes walking away
saves hours of thinking what to say

again there is peace
after war and torment
to surrender oneself

the universe, a relentless poet
reads and writes verses
with impeccable rhyme

with choices half chance
enjoy your dance
to music only the lucky hear

unexpected misfortune
drafts killer survival notes
in a lost art form

battered alchemist hands
finally doing what they love
lead into gold

little steps
build sand into castles
persistence the glue that binds

roses bloom in time
to show all that need to see
their warm bedroom

a pretty weed
felt abnormally high
in the company of roses

the bee took glee
in observing symmetry
it once knew as normal

101

a verse so brilliant
it admired its own rhyme
and uplifted its soul

in a letter, I
explain myself
describing the path to nirvana

i, ii, iii
we accept and grow slowly
all to a less tragic end

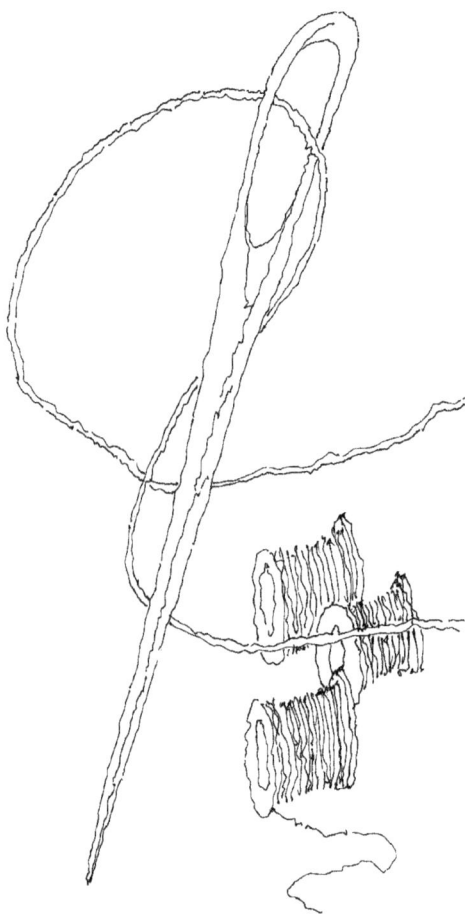

requests satisfied
with a view to happiness
tack on one more stairway plank

spend and save with ease
open hands can receive
desert sand

a happy family
with few possessions
and a big heart

caution the bad sprout
for it may uproot the house
through natural choice or nurture

many a young snake
takes too long finding comfort
in its own skin

poor, unhappy emerald
that would not admit
its flawed perfection

deep tickling flute pipes
echo against the still lake
into the dusky horizon

the judgemental show
an intriguing dislike
for mirrors and reflection

accepting yourself
exactly as you are
is humiliating

don't hurt the oyster
unless it's your nature,
oh, pearls before swine…

stray fish
from a different school of thought
learn from water

the best things in life
obviously include neither simple lives
nor chocolate

the smart make moves
and pay more tax
whilst the slow rest secure

crooked thinking
of devious minds
rescue a world of mediocrity

happy cows
eating grass
smile as they ruminate

oh darling
give the poor waitress a tip
it may improve her day

today the sun shines
tomorrow it may hide
behind its clouds or yours

111

neither pathetic, nor arrogant
revolving doors
meet life at eye level

the lion followed
the fearless mouse
after seeing what it could do

some self-flattery
that the world will copy
and move toward a greater good

at some point
the ocean appears calm and still
the focus rests on waves

the happy cat
plays ball and licks its paws
knowing it could be much worse

appearance deceives
what intellect perceives
as still waters

dreams matter
in the trauma of a short life
sleep well, sweet child

enjoy the good life
  as this is no free ride,
    your time will come

              adonis rich
                could marry a witch
                  subject to broomstick abuse

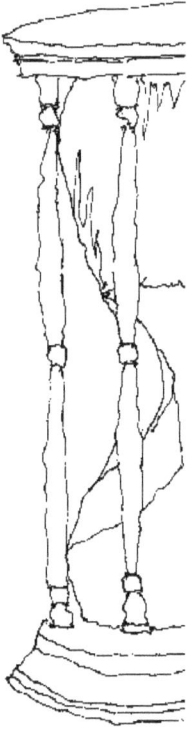

smart fools who test
the universe's memory
will find it always passes

tit for tat
when you least expect
by Little Prince Machiavelli

think and act
for atomic particles react
to make things balance

mercurial nature
mars the best laid plans
to create opportunity

the selfish universe
hogs the pleasure
of your thug being mugged

nature follows
a path of least resistance
when intellect rests its influence

for reasons unreasonable
even ingrown toenails
lead the world to calm balance

the universe knows best
how to achieve its own salvation,
perhaps.

the universe with
its wicked sense of humour
amuses itself

an opportunistic universe
consumes fruit in karma's purse
without caution

exact revenge in the dark,
from behind, and by surprise,
ninja turtle

when natures collide
the universe forces its hand
poor errand boy

in a world ruled by perception
the truth is self-aware

        on flat earth
        belief in heaven's circle
        rules men and conquers

wandering and lost
in a world of mirages
disguised as fleeting truths

        sooner or later
        the truth will confess
        as different as it may be

with exception free understanding
a universe contains its mystery

snobs, yobs and joe bloggs
in a machine just like cogs,
all in their place

a universe fully explained
shows off with brilliant inconsistency

brittle, pink rose petal
flowing, calm soft metal
it all never works always

a twist of fate
converts love to hate
but for the wise

listen to me
for I am the oracle
said the coin to itself

clever eyes that see
what they will
don't tear the veil of clarity

without tinted glasses
and memories passes
there can be but one truth

gods and demons
playfully tease and claim
revenge between the sheets

thinkers seated
on the gates of heaven
are beckoned home

knowing better and worse
the more or less smart
compare with caution

yet another archer
in heaven's army
blinded with foresight

experience grows
        normal boundaries
                until they are erased

        an insignificant speck
        in a vast universe
        realises its importance

a floating moment of clarity
born of random precision
desires to be unique

gazing horizons
every passing dusk and dawn,
victory is one

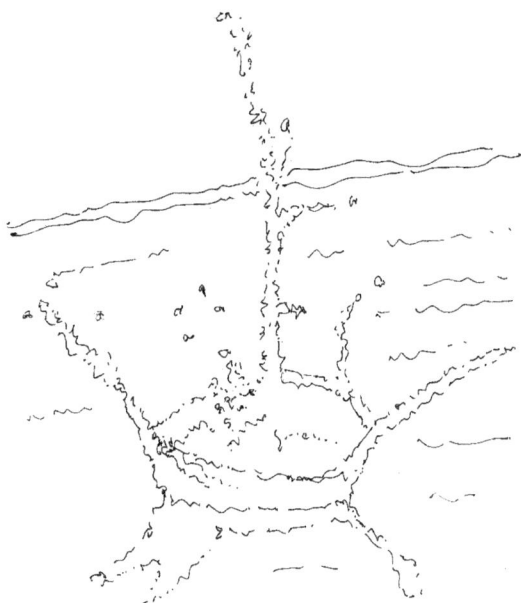

glance the shadows cast
distracting the long and past
comfort seeks high noon

a pebble's simple thought
in its surroundings caught
completely aware

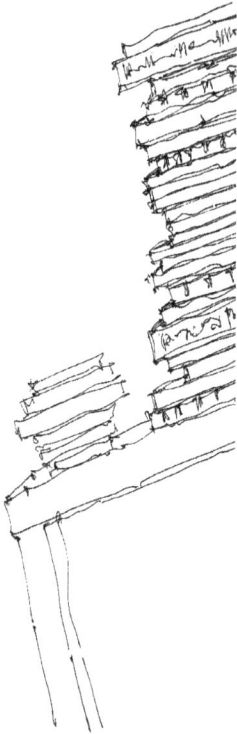

silence natural mystic
people who know more
are almost present

rarely, I find myself
at a loss for words
but what can I say now?

some silly blurb here
quite random and confusing
finds meaning at home

the simple truth
is that words cannot describe
its simplicity

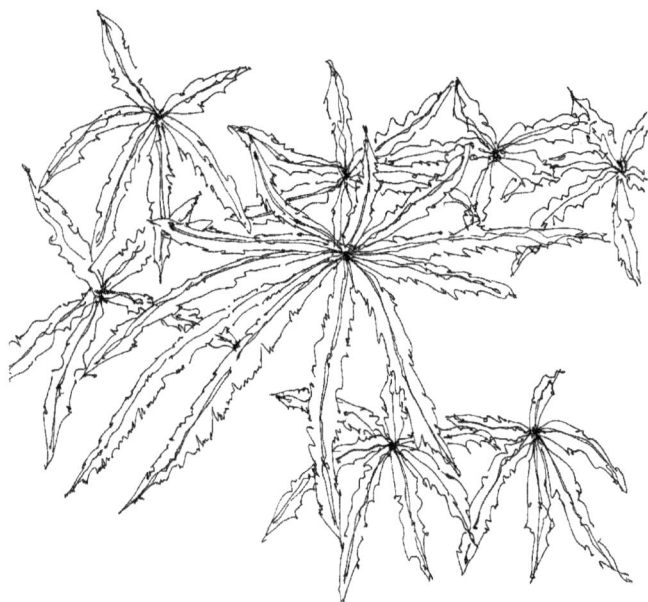

that special point
where normal irritations vanish
is a welcome home

finally, the bow
accepts what was always
the destiny of the arrow

the pebbles smiled
up at the penguin,
all feeling superior

scatterlings of africa
united under a special sky
invisible to strangers

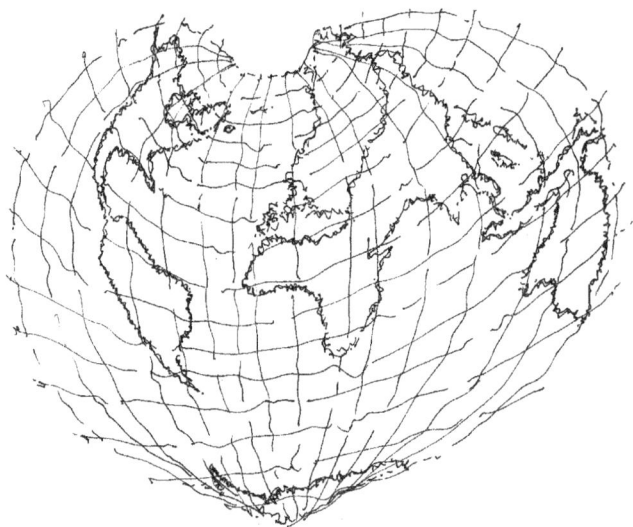

a spirit free
to roam the universe
finds a cosy corner

www.ingramcontent.com/pod-product-compliance
Lightning Source LLC
LaVergne TN
LVHW011237080426
835509LV00005B/542